Weekly Planner and Note Pad

Organize Every Day!

Activinotes

Activinotes

DAILY JOURNALS, PLANNERS, NOTEBOOKS AND OTHER BLANK BOOKS

I0110543

January	February	March

April	May	June

July	August	September

October	November	December

Important Notes

Weekly Planner and Notepad

Week of:

Remarks	Monday	Tuesday	Wednesday

	Thursday	Friday	Saturday	Sunday

Notes

_____

_____

_____

_____

_____

_____

_____

_____

_____

_____

_____

_____

_____

_____

_____

_____

_____

_____

_____

_____

_____

_____

Notes

Weekly Planner and Notepad

Week of:

Remarks	Monday	Tuesday	Wednesday

Thursday	Friday	Saturday	Sunday

Notes

_____

_____

_____

_____

_____

_____

_____

_____

_____

_____

_____

_____

_____

_____

_____

_____

_____

_____

_____

_____

_____

_____

Notes

Weekly Planner and Notepad

Week of:

Remarks	Monday	Tuesday	Wednesday

Thursday	Friday	Saturday	Sunday

Notes

Notes

Weekly Planner and Notepad

Week of:

Remarks	Monday	Tuesday	Wednesday

Thursday	Friday	Saturday	Sunday

Notes

Notes

Weekly Planner and Notepad

Week of:

Remarks	Monday	Tuesday	Wednesday

Thursday	Friday	Saturday	Sunday

Notes

Notes

Weekly Planner and Notepad

Week of:

Remarks	Monday	Tuesday	Wednesday

Thursday	Friday	Saturday	Sunday

Notes

Notes

_____

_____

_____

_____

_____

_____

_____

_____

_____

_____

_____

_____

_____

_____

_____

_____

_____

_____

_____

_____

_____

_____

_____

Weekly Planner and Notepad

Week of:

Remarks	Monday	Tuesday	Wednesday

Thursday	Friday	Saturday	Sunday

Notes

Notes

Weekly Planner and Notepad

Week of:

Remarks	Monday	Tuesday	Wednesday

Thursday	Friday	Saturday	Sunday

Notes

Notes

Weekly Planner and Notepad

Week of:

Remarks	Monday	Tuesday	Wednesday

Thursday	Friday	Saturday	Sunday

Notes

Notes

Weekly Planner and Notepad

Week of:

Remarks	Monday	Tuesday	Wednesday

Thursday	Friday	Saturday	Sunday

Notes

Notes

Weekly Planner and Notepad

Week of:

Remarks	Monday	Tuesday	Wednesday

Thursday	Friday	Saturday	Sunday

Notes

Notes

Weekly Planner and Notepad

Week of:

Remarks	Monday	Tuesday	Wednesday

Thursday	Friday	Saturday	Sunday

Notes

Notes

_____

_____

_____

_____

_____

_____

_____

_____

_____

_____

_____

_____

_____

_____

_____

_____

_____

_____

_____

_____

Weekly Planner and Notepad

Week of:

Remarks	Monday	Tuesday	Wednesday

Thursday	Friday	Saturday	Sunday

Notes

Notes

_____

_____

_____

_____

_____

_____

_____

_____

_____

_____

_____

_____

_____

_____

_____

_____

_____

_____

Weekly Planner and Notepad

Week of:

Remarks	Monday	Tuesday	Wednesday

Thursday	Friday	Saturday	Sunday

Notes

Notes

Weekly Planner and Notepad

Week of:

Remarks	Monday	Tuesday	Wednesday

Thursday	Friday	Saturday	Sunday

Notes

Notes

Weekly Planner and Notepad

Week of:

Remarks	Monday	Tuesday	Wednesday

Thursday	Friday	Saturday	Sunday

Notes

Notes

Weekly Planner and Notepad

Week of:

Remarks	Monday	Tuesday	Wednesday

	Thursday	Friday	Saturday	Sunday

Notes

Notes

Weekly Planner and Notepad

Week of:

Remarks	Monday	Tuesday	Wednesday

Thursday	Friday	Saturday	Sunday

Notes

_____

_____

_____

_____

_____

_____

_____

_____

_____

_____

_____

_____

_____

_____

_____

_____

_____

_____

_____

_____

Notes

Weekly Planner and Notepad

Week of:

Remarks	Monday	Tuesday	Wednesday

Thursday	Friday	Saturday	Sunday

Notes

Notes

Weekly Planner and Notepad

Week of:

Remarks	Monday	Tuesday	Wednesday

Thursday	Friday	Saturday	Sunday

Notes

Notes

Weekly Planner and Notepad

Week of:

Remarks	Monday	Tuesday	Wednesday

Thursday	Friday	Saturday	Sunday

Notes

Notes

Weekly Planner and Notepad

Week of:

Remarks	Monday	Tuesday	Wednesday

Thursday	Friday	Saturday	Sunday

Notes

Notes

Weekly Planner and Notepad

Week of:

Remarks	Monday	Tuesday	Wednesday

Thursday	Friday	Saturday	Sunday

Notes

Notes

Weekly Planner and Notepad

Week of:

Remarks	Monday	Tuesday	Wednesday

Thursday	Friday	Saturday	Sunday

Notes

Notes

Weekly Planner and Notepad

Week of:

Remarks	Monday	Tuesday	Wednesday

Thursday	Friday	Saturday	Sunday

Notes

_____

_____

_____

_____

_____

_____

_____

_____

_____

_____

_____

_____

_____

_____

_____

_____

_____

_____

_____

_____

_____

Notes

_____

_____

_____

_____

_____

_____

_____

_____

_____

_____

_____

_____

_____

_____

_____

_____

_____

_____

_____

_____

_____

Notes

Notes